Practicing Perfect Love

By

Dr. Don Burchfield

ISBN: 0-75963-436-X

This book is printed on acid free paper.

1stBooks - rev. 6/22/01

CONTENTS

AUTHOR'S NOTE

You have made a choice to look at the words in this book. By making this choice, you have confirmed a desire in you to change something. What you want to change really does not matter at all. What matters most is that you want to change. I am glad you have taken the time to think about love and how love changes everything. Think about these words that I try to live by-no man will ever be moved to action without faith, and no man's faith is real until it moves him to action.

Please act now and read <u>Practicing Perfect Love.</u>

When things go wrong, as they sometime will,
When the road you're trudging seems all up hill,
When the funds are low and the debts are high,
And you want to smile, but you have to sigh,
When care is pressing you down a bit,
Rest, if you must-but don't you quit.

Success is failure turned inside out—
The silver tint of the clouds of doubt—
And you never can tell how close you are,
It may be near when it seems afar;
So stick to the fight then you're hardest hit—
It's when things seem worse that you mustn't quit.

Anonymous

Don, hope this will do the job, make any changes that you or your publishers think is relevant, keeping in mind what I passed on to you previously about the Traditions of my Program. Uncle **Walter**

Foreword

I am the Uncle of the Author of this booklet and am honored to have been asked to write a few words about the booklet.

In my quest for peace of mind and serenity I have tried many avenues as I'm sure the reader of this booklet has. My nephew is the oldest son of my sister and therefore I am familiar with his search for "Perfect Love". Coming from the same type of family we both understand that circumstances outside of our control restrict us from seeking during our early childhood years without being laughed at. I personally have been involved with self help groups, since I was 45 years old, 15 years ago now. I have been a Salesman during the past 31 years, just retiring and I assure you the concepts in this booklet would be meaningful to all walks of life. It has been my experience that the words in this booklet will enable the seeker of peace and serenity to find it with the enactment of Forgiveness of others, even perhaps more paramount than Forgiveness of self. Although one without the other will bring no peace of mind.

I encourage the reader to explore this booklet with an open mind and find the serenity in their life that I have found in mine by using the concepts outlined in this booklet.

Don, I thank you for asking me to write this and am glad that God has put you back into my life after over 25 years of being out of contact. Reader's do not let the word God, scare you from trying the concepts of the book, when I use the word God, I'm referring to God Orderly Direction, which your life will take on by using the tools in this book.

I wish you and Don all "Perfect Love".

In Gratitude
Walter Whitecotton
Don's Uncle

A READING FROM <u>**THE PROPHET**</u>

Your pain is the breaking of the shell that encloses your understanding.

Even as the stone of the fruit must break, that its heart may stand in the sun, so must you know pain.

And could you keep your heart in wonder at the daily miracles of your life, your pain would not seem less wondrous than your joy.

And you would accept the seasons of your heart, even as you have always accepted the seasons that pass over your fields.

And you would watch with serenity through the winters of your grief.

Much of your pain is self-chosen.

It is the bitter potion by which the physician within you heals your sick self.

Therefore trust the physician, and drink his remedy in silence and tranquility.

For his hand, though heavy and hard, is guided by the tender hand of the Unseen,

And the cup he brings, though it burn your lips, has been fashioned of the clay which the Potter has moistened with His own sacred tears.

Kahil Gibran

Forward to "Practicing Perfect Love".

As a therapist, psychologist and counselor for the past fifteen years I have encountered only a few books that strike and move the emotions and the intellect as does Dr. Burchfield's "Practicing Perfect Love".

This book helps bridge that elusive gap between thought and action in such a simple yet meaningful way that in reading it one cannot help but begin to see a new way to open the mind and heart for making a positive change in their life.

The reader will feel the energy and emotion of this book from the very first paragraph and before the last page they will have seen and felt a new and brighter way to view themselves and the world around them.

I would recommend "Practicing Perfect Love" to be read by people of all ages and all walks of life, and especially to my colleagues and friends who practice the art of helping. It is one of those rare books that gives you something almost tangible; something you can feel. Something you can use. Read it.

February, 16, 2001
Stanley L. Eden, Psy.D.

Dr. Eden is a licensed psychologist practicing in Phoenix, Arizona. He has over fifteen years experience in treating psychological and substance abuse problems with teens, adults and families.

A READING FROM <u>THE PROPHET</u>

Your hearts know in silence the secrets of the days and the nights.

But your ears thirst for the sound of your heart's knowledge.

You would know in words that which you have always known in thought.

You would touch with your fingers the naked body of your dreams.

And it is well you should.

The hidden well-spring of your soul must needs rise and run murmuring to the sea;

And the treasure of your infinite depths would be revealed to your eyes.

But let there be no scales to weight your unknown treasure;

And seek not the depths of your knowledge with staff or sounding line.

For self is a sea boundless and measureless.

Say not, "I have found truth," but rather, "I have found a truth."

Practicing Perfect Love

You can find an explanation of how you can be free from the control of your past experiences and thoughts and live in peace and joy today.

Love and forgiveness are clearly illustrated as the means by which you can change your life now by making the right choices. Fear is the emotion that cuts down your ability to act, even to love, that threatens bad consequences. Guilt is self-distrust, nonacceptance of self; and unforgiveness is nonacceptance of both self and others.

When you are affected by guilt, fear, and unforgiveness, you will find that these emotions are harmful to you, that they cause pain. Love and forgiveness are the antidotes to these harmful results. Past conditions that contributed to your having pain cannot be changed, but the way you think now can be changed, enabling you to live today and tomorrow without this pain. You can begin now learning a new way of thinking that will change how your future life will be.

No matter where you go, to the shopping center, to social activities, to church or even at home, there are people who are experiencing pain. Note how each of these people look unhappy. When you look into their faces, you see their depression, sickness, hopelessness, discouragement, sorrow, evident in their expressions.

Look now at how your own face expresses itself. If in pain, you not only can feel it, but you also can see it.

Everyone is in need of love so they no longer must live in pain. All of us must do our best to help these unhappy ones in their struggle in life. The past has handed them, and even possibly you, the worst that life can offer. Bringing

*Fear is the
emotion that
cuts down your
ability to act,
even to love,
that threatens
bad consequences.*

peace and joy to them, and yourself, will happen as the principal of practicing perfect love unfolds in you.

The past is to learn from, but never to glory in. I am grateful that through my pain, I found a way to live in peace and to maintain this peace. This booklet will help you see how each day you can determine your peace and have freedom from pain. I developed this practice of "perfect love" through my own meditation, reading and personal experiences. It is this practice that will keep my pain, and yours, from ever returning in such a way as to destroy any area of our lives.

Practicing perfect loves is treating everyone as innocent, even those who cause you pain. You understand that fear and guilt are causing this attack. Second, you direct the peace within you toward the one causing pain. When you direct this peace to the other person, you are not allowing this attack to affect your peace and joy. When you expect nothing in return for your attitude of peace, love happens. This love, then, will free you to forgive the one causing pain. This forgiveness prevents you from having pain. These are the steps in practicing perfect love.

We have arrived at a oneness with love. We see peace not only as a state of being but a vital force that we can enjoy, control, and project. We replace guilt and blame and declare innocence for ourselves and others.

Perfect love in us is being manifested by our actions, thoughts and words. Perfect love, loves through us. We will not ever be without mistakes and failures. We will always have areas in our lives to deal with. When we love, we are allowing perfect love to happen freely, resulting in perfect peace. This is our goal, to keep pressing on each day, discovering how we can live at peace.

Practicing
perfect loves is
treating
everyone as
innocent, even
those who
cause you pain.

Start at the point of whatever is troubling you, bringing hurt, causing pain, and take the action necessary to change it. Focus on what needs to be changed. You do not need to waste energy on why this is happening, just that it is to be changed. Develop trust in love, see the cause of pain and hurt as innocent. Direct peace to this cause. Just make sure you see the outside force of fear and guilt as the only guilty ones. When you direct peace and see the cause as innocent, you have no reason to hurt or be in pain, because there is no need to react in a way that would bring fear, guilt, depression, resentment, and unforgiveness. Peace is experienced when you practice perfect love.

All of us want peace and love. When we are convinced that the result of practicing perfect love is peace and love, then we will begin trying it.

We all want less conflict, fear, stress and depression in our lives. But so much of the time we create our own conflict, fear, stress and depression. We think we can be right by proving someone else wrong. We think there are people who deserve to lose because of their behavior and that the pain they receive is justice. We try to increase love with one person by excluding others. We do these things and we do not want pain for ourselves or others, but we do not know whether we can do what it takes to practice perfect love. For perfect love does require sacrifice. There can be no love without costing something. Discover how you are to love.

Innocence

Practicing perfect love is to search for innocence so we can free ourselves of pain, grief, depression, guilt and other

*We all want
less conflict,
fear, stress and
depression in
our lives.*

forms of fear. See this cause of pain as innocent. Anything innocent brings no harm.

Practicing perfect love sees all who attack in thought, word or deed as innocent, but controlled by fear and guilt. Guilt and fear at times can control us in ways that would bring pain. When we see "all" not guilty and as ones who need love, perfect love happens. The key word here is "all".

Fear

Perfect love casts out all fear. We will fear until perfect love replaces this fear. Perfect love is the power that casts out fear and the results caused by fear.

Everyone feared, but not everyone has to fear. Fear limits us. Fear takes life from us, love casts out that fear. Life is given back to us by loving. Fear takes our peace. "Peace...the result of love casting out fear."

Forgiveness

Practicing perfect love requires practicing peace of mind and forgiveness. Peace of mind refuses to be angry in such a way as to cause pain and bring conflict upon yourself. Refuse to be angry, be at peace. Forgiveness clears our conscience. A clear conscience is a mind at peace. Nothing can clear the conscience except forgiveness.

This is where so many miss the whole meaning of love. Many books are written to help you deal with guilt, fear and unforgiveness. Very few of them require the cleansing of the conscience before you can heal yourself.

*Forgiveness
clears our
conscience.
A clear
conscience
is a mind
at peace.*

Say not, "I have found the path of the soul," but rather, "I have met the would walking upon my path."

For the soul walks upon all paths.

The soul walks not upon a line, neither does it grow like a reed.

The soul unfolds itself, like a lotus of countless petals.

Kahil Gibran

You can only forgive others as you have forgiven yourself. When you know you are forgiven, you can forgive others and be healed. No one can offer healing until peace is made with yourself. Practicing perfect love comes from a heart that is forgiven and forgiving.

"Forgive me. Please forgive me." How often we find ourselves pleading for forgiveness. Here on earth we do not have role models that forgive unconditionally, hence it is hard to understand this kind of forgiveness. When you love yourself, you can forgive yourself, then forgiving others is possible.

We know we are to forgive, and we can, if we discipline ourselves to live at peace and see all people as innocent. The love and forgiveness that prevents pain will follow as needed.

When forgiving, you do not need to know who is at fault or who should ask forgiveness, just simply forgive. Forgiving is letting go. Just be willing to forgive and give up negative feelings. Let them go and go on with your life. If you make this a part of your life, you will be at peace and not living in turmoil. Forgiveness is a gentle refusal to defend ourselves against love any longer.

Forgiveness is the way to true health and happiness. By not judging, but seeing all as innocent, you can let the past go. This peace from seeing all as innocent can be directed to others.

The past can create negative feelings that hurt. To prevent the past from repeating in the future, the past must be let go. When you let go of the past, you have only now. What you do now can bring love and heal pain and anger. So much of our lives have been so painful that just to think that life could be different brings excitement, joy and peace.

When forgiving,
you do not need to
know who is at fault
or who should ask
forgiveness,
just simply forgive.

Eliminating anger, resentment and stress is not a dream, but a reality when practicing perfect love.

Any emotion or thought that distresses you will begin to lose its power on your mind when it is examined peacefully. Pause whenever you are having difficulty releasing your mind from being upset, and look directly and in detail at the contents of your mind. If you let fear attack this peaceful thought, you will stop forgiving, and the reaction to this attack will bring you negative results, instead of the results that come from practicing perfect love.

When we evaluate our behavior and become self-critical or unkind to ourselves, we make our world angry and unloving. These thoughts create an unloving attitude. When we retrain our minds to look past these thoughts, we can see ourselves as we desire ourselves to be and then we can act on what we now see. This change of thinking will reduce pain. It can be difficult because change is hard.

The thoughts we think and the direction we take actually determine if we want to live or die. The world does not have to change before we can be happy, peaceful and thoughtful of others. The only thing that has to change is our attitude. Situations do not usually change. We are the ones who change so that we can handle the situation.

When we allow fear to be replaced by love, the peace that replaces this fear will give a clear conscience and peace of mind. The mind can be tormented by fear and guilt and unforgiveness. Love conquers this fear, removes guilt and forgives so the conscience can be clear.

Quiet your mind and desire the peace more than anything else. Give thanks for the pain and give love to any area that is producing pain. This is practicing perfect love.

The thoughts
we think and
the direction
we take
actually
determine if we
want to live or
die.

Thought and Thinking

Our feelings about ourselves, our past, our future and the present are determined by a thought. If you do not like what you feel, remember it is determined by a thought, and thoughts are learned; therefore, you can determine to change the thought to one that expresses how you want to feel.

We think thoughts and speak words that reveal how we feel. How we relate to others and how we react to what others say and do is controlled by what we think and speak. We are the ones who have power over our thoughts. With this in mind, begin now to think the way you want to feel.

Stay away from thoughts that bring pain. Refuse thoughts that make you feel hopeless or that change is impossible.

If you do not like the way you feel about something, that is a signal that change is necessary.

Think of your mind as only a tool that is yours to use to bring the results you want. The mind is not running your life. Allow love to be the example to follow. Train your mind after this example. You are in control of the mind. You determine what the mind thinks. As you train the mind to think in the way necessary to practice perfect love, you will be living this love as a way of life.

The mind can be retrained. In this fact lies our freedom. Unlearn the thinking that keeps you a prisoner of your own insecurities.

To think positive is very difficult for many because people have misused the concept of positive thinking. Many have taught concepts concerning positive thinking

*Stay away from
thoughts that
bring pain.
Refuse
thoughts that
make you feel
hopeless or
that change is
impossible.*

A READING FROM <u>THE PROPHET</u>

Your joy is your sorrow unmasked.

And the selfsame from which your laughter rises was oftentimes filled with your tears.

And how else can it be?

The deeper that sorrow carves into your being, the more joy you can contain.

Is not the cup that holds your wine the very cup that was burned in the potter's oven?

And is not the lute that soothes your spirit, the very wood that was hollowed with knives?

When you are joyous, look deep into your heart and you shall find it is only that which has given you sorrow that is giving you joy.

When you are sorrowful look again in your heart, and you shall see that in truth you are weeping for that which has been your delight.

Some of you say, "Joy is greater than sorrow," and others say, "Nay, sorrow is the greater."

But I say unto you, they are inseparable.

that are very unrealistic. The true concept of thinking in a positive manner is realistic. There really are only two ways to think, positively or negatively. If you are not having positive thoughts, you then are having negative thoughts. There is not anything in the middle, since all thoughts determine action in some way or another.

Each thought you think will affect you in a positive or negative way. All of us practice positive thinking even when we are not actually acknowledging it as such.

Thinking positively is practicing perfect love in its highest form. Thinking positively is being in control of your thoughts and your life.

We must be consistent in everything we think and say and do. We must be unified within ourselves so we find true peace. If we are not consistent in our thinking, we will progress slowly. It is important that you keep at peace so that, when others try to bring pain, you can respond by loving and seeing them as innocent.

With a clear conscience, you are able to direct the peace within yourself to others so that they can be seen as the ones who need love. Even when we are practicing peace of mind, we are still challenged each day to keep peaceful.

Anger

Why do we strike out at others in anger, with words, thoughts or deeds? These actions are meant to hurt. We find ourselves reacting to what people say or how they act. When we do this, we hate how we act so we punish ourselves by seeing ourselves as bad. This kind of attitude will continue being repeated until we change this cycle.

*We must be
consistent in
everything we
think and say
and do. We
must be unified
within ourselves
so we find true
peace.*

Stop, look and listen to yourself. There is a better way? Say what needs to be said in a way that does not bring pain. Keep at peace, but also correct the situation that is causing the conflict in the first place.

You are not to allow these situations, that would normally upset you, to go without attention. Deal with them, but do it in a way that is peaceful and painless. This will bring the results needed and also keep you from hurting yourself. Practicing perfect love does not mean you are to not use firmness and discipline. It only means that, to accomplish the results needed, you should act in a way that is painless.

The more you give out anger, the more times you will respond in anger. This will just repeat itself as long as you continue to react in this fashion.

You allow your power or authority over yourself to be taken from you when you blame others instead of taking responsibility yourself. This power has been given you to provide a life of peace. When we try to rid ourselves of guilt by blaming others, then we only increase guilt and weaken authority we have in love.

If you are in touch with yourself and are aware of your own emotions and thoughts, anger and guilt, you will be less likely to be angry and blame or project guilt on others. This will make you happier because by being aware, you will not transmit these same feelings to others. Others will be spared more pain and in return spare others from pain. You make others free of pain in the same manner as you create pain in others, by the way you treat them.

You are giving away your power or authority over the cause of pain and hurt when you blame others for what happens to you. You allow them to reduce your ability to take control when you direct your energy to blaming.

19

*It is difficult to
accept the fact
that you are the
cause of the
feelings that
take away your
joy in life when
you allow the
pain and hurt
directed at you
to affect you.*

Do not blame others. Assume the responsibility to love, to forgive no matter who may be at fault. It really does not matter who is at fault, as long as you do not allow pain and hurt to be directed to or felt by you. Take control and practice perfect love, and you will avoid i the results that remove the peace you enjoy.

The truth is you really are in control of loving or not loving. You do decide whether or not you will love. It is difficult to accept the fact that you are the cause of the feelings that take away your joy in life when you allow the pain and hurt directed at you to affect you. If you can create your own fear and guilt, it stands to reason that you can also create your own peace and love. You are the cause of your own reactions to things directed to harm your peace and joy. The truth can scare us, but it can also heal us.

By practicing perfect love, you do not have to allow others to make you feel negative about yourself. You can change how you feel about yourself by practicing perfect love.

Many voices are pulling for your attention every day. Many choices are to be made as the day goes by. Determine whether any of these voices or choices bring pain and hurt and then determine that, if they do, you will practice perfect love.

Sometimes you make promises to yourself that you will never do "this" again. Then something happens and you do whatever "this" was. While making the promises, you had good intentions, but the time you made this promise, usually was when you had just done "this" At the time, you did not like what it was that made you promise. The only bad thing about the promise was that "this" came up again and you gave into "this" The feeling of guilt creeps up and

Dr. Don Burchfield

When you
speak and think
the truth about
yourself, you
sleep better,
feel better,
and have peace
within.

you feel like such a bad person because you did not keep your promise.

Do not promise, just commit to try. If each time you want to change an action, thought, or word, just commit to try. If you do not succeed, then try again. There is no reason to feel guilty from trying. Keep trying and you will succeed. Keep promising and you will keep breaking promises.

Self-Understanding

Change the way you think. Speak and act by stopping, looking, and listening. Decide when it is necessary to practice perfect love.

When you speak and think the truth about yourself, you sleep better, feel better, and have peace within. This peace comes because you are no longer repressing guilt. You are no longer deceiving yourself. You are no longer critical of yourself. This is the result of practicing perfect love. The truth about yourself will not hurt as much as denial of the truth.

When you realize and accept that you are not perfect in all areas and that no one will treat you as perfect at all times, you have helped to keep yourself from unnecessary pain. This honesty with yourself and others will strengthen you. Honesty will help you admit your thoughts, feelings and actions that are not helpful. Once you admit to being imperfect, change is possible. Now you will do what must be done to raise your self-respect and self-esteem. The truth sets you free.

Perfection is a desire within all of us. This is a good desire as long as it is kept within realistic terms. Being

*Perfection is a
desire within
all of us. This
is a good
desire as long
as it is kept
within realistic
terms.*

Together they come, and when one sits alone with you at your board, remember that the other is asleep upon your bed.

Verily, you are suspended like scales between your sorrow and your joy.

Only when you are empty are you at standstill and balanced.

When the treasure-keeper lifts you to weigh his gold and his silver, needs must your joy or your sorrow rise or fall.

Kahil Gibran

unrealistic creates pain. Living life as it is, and making mistakes and wrong choices, does not mean you are not perfect. Perfection comes as you allow your love to be seen within you. Love is perfect. Love does not prevent us from making mistakes, but does perfect in us the ability to love perfectly.

Improving yourself is a good desire as long as you realize that it takes time. Do not expect more than is possible or you will create guilt. Guilt is developed in large from your desire to be without flaws. To be perfect all the time in all areas needs to be recognized as unrealistic.

We are not perfect; we are human. We will always make mistakes, make wrong decisions. Practicing perfect love does not mean that you are perfect, it is letting perfect love determine how you treat others. You will never be perfect and to think you will, will only create guilt.

Love continues to see us as innocent. This innocence declares us not guilty. This forgiveness creates our peace. Our practice of perfect love must be daily practice. This is a daily discipline of remaining in control to love, and remain healed of pain and live with our minds at peace.

Perfect love must be practiced. If you do not practice then you lose the skill. Anything practiced becomes easier; less practiced, the harder it is to accomplish. You must keep at it daily. With each small change, another door opens for us to enter. Each day, practice this perfect love as if a brick wall needs to be removed, one brick at a time. To remove the entire wall, you must stay at it daily. Love never fails. Love is there when needed. Determine to love every time necessary to prevent yourself from becoming unforgiving, fearful or guilty.

*Every emotion
that we have,
such as guilt
and fear, serves
a purpose.*

Practice perfect love on yourself and positive changes will take place in every area of your life. Loving ourselves works miracles in our lives.

Directing this love toward ourselves changes how we treat ourselves. We feel worthy. When we feel needed and useful, healing happens. When we feel as though we are making a difference and that our lives do count for something, our entire being-body, mind, and spirit becomes involved in the results of practicing perfect love on ourselves. We become able to deal with our pain and our emotions.

Guilt and Fear

Every emotion that we have, such as guilt and fear, serves a purpose. When guilt and fear bring pain and bondage, then the purpose served is a warning signal. This is a cry for help. Being aware of this purpose of our emotions, and responding in a helpful way, makes guilt and fear, in this case, necessary.

To some, fear is a fact of life that must be accepted. It is true, fear is part of life but it is never to be accepted as a fact of life. To be a fact of life would mean that it would be impossible to remove fear. Here is exciting news. Fear can become history. If we practice perfect love, peace can be a fact of life.

Being critical, feeling guilt, and/or having fear creates the major problems in our lives. If you really believe this, then don't you think you need to change? Do not allow these behaviors to continue to punish you. Just because you now are experiencing criticism, guilt, and fear does not mean you have to continue to endure such feelings.

*Accept
yourself.
Forgive
yourself and
believe you are
changing
because you
are thinking
differently
about yourself.*

God is love, and the one who abides in love abides in God, and God abides in Him, love is perfected with us...there is no fear in love, but perfect love casts out fear, because fear involves punishment, and the one who fears is not perfected in love.

Apostle John

Do not feel you are a bad person because of your thoughts. This only makes you feel worse. You are where you are because of the way you think about yourself. Decide how you want to feel about yourself and feel that way by seeing yourself as innocent.

Direct peace to those feelings you do not like. Love yourself now, even with these feelings you do not like about yourself. Accept yourself. Forgive yourself and believe you are changing because you are thinking differently about yourself.

Thoughts in the past do not have to be repeated in the now. It does not matter how long this negative pattern existed. Your past is that way because you were not aware that you could have changed what happened, so you are innocent. You have power to change when you know what you want the change to be. Direct innocence, peace, love and forgiveness toward yourself by practicing perfect love.

You can change, even if you find it hard to see yourself as innocent. When you and I project guilt on others to reduce our own guilt and find it only increases our guilt, does not help. Guilt projected tries to shift the blame rather than letting it go. Projection is a form of attack. We are only punishing ourselves as we blame and project guilt. There is no other way to be free from guilt other than letting go and seeing ourselves as innocent.

Guilt and fear are devastating to us. We try blaming and projecting guilt on others to free ourselves. We even deny this guilt or fear. Denial pushes us even deeper into the grip of guilt or fear. This creates even more pain and depression.

We seek punishment for ourselves as we act on thoughts that contribute to guilt. We become angry at ourselves. We hope this anger will cover up guilt that

Anxiety is energy.
Energy must be
released.

Release of anxious
energy becomes a
lifestyle of self-help.
Holistic (needs all parts)
i.e. eating right, sleeping,
exercise, vitamins,
positive thoughts,
reduce caffiene,
reduce sugar,
counselling, medication
(if necessary.)

comes from wanting to do or think thoughts we know are not good.

I feel anger; therefore, I feel guilt because I feel anger. I feel fear because of what will happen to me from guilt. If we find peace, it will free us from this pain.

Guilt, allowed to continue to bring pain, can result in cancer, heart failure, accidents, addictions, suicides and murders. When we get rid of this guilt and replace it with love, much of the pain in our lives will disappear.

Understand why you feel guilty. You can free yourself from guilt as you acknowledge your hatred and become aware of why you feel this guilt. This is the beginning of love and forgiveness of yourself.

When you face your guilt you begin to free yourself from the prison of pain. Past rejections and past hurts are the pain felt today, which can disappear as your practice perfect love on yourself.

Telling others the truth for your guilt can bring fear, the fear of losing their love and respect. Forgive yourself by admitting the truth to yourself. Forgive others and do not think that everyone has to be told. Some things are better kept to yourself.

Feel the fear, but then realize that this fear has no control and go ahead and do what the fear is trying to keep you from doing. You know whether it is healthy fear or not. The fear that brings bondage, pain and hurt is an unhealthy fear. Go ahead and do what the unhealthy fear says not to do. Doing it anyway frees you from the control by this fear. You can do whatever it was when you have no reason to fear it. Be at peace with what you feared.

Handling fear is moving from a position of pain to one of power or authority. Negative thoughts take away your

Negative thoughts take away your power, positive thoughts bring power and authority and control back into your life.

power, positive thoughts bring power and authority and control back into your life.

Love Replaces Pain

Fear and pain disappear as we give love now and forgive the past. Perfect love casts out fear and all the results of fear, such as guilt and unforgiveness.

Man's choice not to love is missing the mark. There is no love in this choice of disobedience. To be at peace and to be whole is created by loving.

The emotion, love, is our natural inheritance and fear is an invention of our minds that affects our conscience. When love casts out fear, our minds are at peace and our conscience cleared through the gift of forgiveness.

You have the power. This power is authority to live in love. You have all the authority or power needed to live in love. All of this power is within you: power over how you perceive the world, over how you react; power to bring about self-growth, power to create joy and satisfaction in your life, the power to act in love and in peace over anything that threatens your healthy self-love. Power and love go together.

You determine how the power or authority will affect your progress of growth. The peace within and love displayed brings growth that removes as much fear, guilt and forgiveness as you desire. Allow love and peace to completely overcome guilt, fear and unforgiveness, since that is what you want.

When we love, we are not afraid of what others might say or do. We see ourselves as love, and others as love so we expect unity with ourselves and others. We start to love

The emotion,
love, is our
natural inheritance
and fear is
an invention
of our minds
that affects
our conscience.

Ask, and it shall be given to you; seek, and you shall find; knock, and it shall be opened to you, for everyone who asks receives, and he who seeks find, and to him who knocks it shall be opened."

Jesus

whenever we choose to accept people without judging them and commence the gentle effort of giving without any thought of getting something in payment.

Love overlooks differences because love notices something far greater, that is how much like each other we are. We see each other as created to love. We begin to lose our fear of others and see each other as harmless. This harmlessness makes the innocence of each other a reality. Seeing one another as innocent reduces the cause of pain.

If love makes you happy and guilt makes you unhappy, them remove guilt. If guilt limits the ability to love, then remove guilt. If facing guilt keeps you from expressing love more honestly, then remove guilt. If guilt makes it more difficult to receive love, then remove guilt. If hate will be removed when guilt is removed then, by all means, remove guilt. Removing guilt is just letting go and giving it up. Removing guilt is taking the guilt you feel and practicing perfect love directed toward this guilt.

The more helpless you feel, the more you need to depend on the power of love. Love is there because you are love. There is power in love. Take a moment now, think of a recent time you felt love. Now allow that feeling to repeat itself. Feel that? That is power. Yes, love has power.

The feeling of helplessness comes when at any time you stop recognizing that you are love and you are made from love, which has no limitations. Power in love knows no limits. Without love, you cannot experience perfect peace, clear conscience, or forgiveness. Now that you are loved perfectly, you can practice perfect love.

We are in this world only to learn and teach love. As long as we are alive, we are to allow our love to extend in a form that others can recognize and receive.

*Love overlooks
differences
because love
notices
something far
greater, that is
how much like
each other we
are.*

When we take the chance to love others, we take the chance of rejection. This rejection can only be felt if the love you offer is not perfect love. Perfect love does not care how it is received. Perfect love is offered no matter what happens. Practicing perfect love cannot be rejected when offered out of a heart filled by perfect love. We were created out of love; to love while here on earth. We are here to love; that is our purpose.

Releasing Emotions

To help you understand this concept, let's imagine that someone or something becomes part of your life and provides a threat or potential pain. When you become aware of what is happening, take control of the situation.

Determine what emotion you are being made to feel, guilt or fear. After you are aware of the emotion you are feeling, ask yourself if you want this feeling changed.

You have four choices; you can suppress, that is, deny the emotion. You can escape, that would be to project or blame the emotion on others. You could express, this is to tell others about your emotions. You could release this emotion.

If you want this emotion changed because you know it will produce pain, then to release it is the only way change can happen.

To release, first make sure the emotion you are feeling is harmless. Also that the situation causing you to experience this emotion is innocent. When you see this situation as harmless, then allow yourself to feel this emotion. Now that you feel it, are you willing to release it

*If you want this
emotion
changed
because you
know it will
produce pain,
then to release it
is the only
way change
can happen.*

Dr. Don Burchfield

As long as I try there is hope.

or let it go? Since it is harmless and the cause is innocent, there is no reason to react.

This emotion wanted to control you and make you do what it wanted, but, by going ahead and feeling it and seeing it as harmless, you were able to let it go. You did not react in a negative harmful way, but a positive helpful way.

To help make this principle of dealing with emotions easier to understand, let us look together at this example.

At times, while writing this booklet, I would feel a strong fear attacking me. This fear was telling me that I was not qualified to write. I had no right to have this booklet read by others. Fear wanted to control me so I would give this up.

I could have suppressed, escaped, expressed or released this emotion of fear. I chose to release this fear so the control would be limited. I saw this fear as harmlessly innocent. This emotion was from outside trying to control my mind. I felt peace because I realized this fear would have no control if I decided not to obey it. By feeling it and letting it go, I practiced perfect love on this fear. I did not allow this emotion to harm me since I gave no power to this fear.

When you consider all emotions that you feel, the result will be that emotions do control our actions and thoughts. The emotions we feel control us in either a positive or negative manner. The choice is how we are controlled.

You cannot stop the control that emotions have, but you do determine the result this control has on you. Being aware of the emotion and the power the emotion can have makes you the one who chooses how you will be affected.

All emotions that we feel require a choice. Once an emotion is felt there is no way you can ignore that emotion.

If you allow the emotion to continue without your control, the effect will be determined by the emotion itself.

If you allow the emotion to continue without your control, the effect will be determined by the emotion itself.

If fear is felt and allowed to continue, then you will experience negative results. These negative results will manifest themselves as guilt, criticism, depression, unforgiveness, resentment or sickness.

When this fear is first felt, take control and you will not have to suffer from these negative results. Being in control, you can feel the fear and let it go before any harmful effects have time to develop within your body.

It is important that you understand this concept and how it works. This booklet expresses this way of thinking and acting. Like anything that becomes a habit or part of your life, control takes time. Usually, when a thought or action is repeated every day for a month, a pattern will be developed that soon becomes the habit you are wanting to establish.

When I decided I wanted to have a regular exercise program to follow, I joined an aerobics class. I made sure that I went everyday for a month. I created a habit of exercise that has not changed in three years. If you practice perfect love daily, it will become a natural way for you to think and act.

I am convinced that if you will do what I have said, you will never again be controlled by anyone or anything, unless you choose to be. Allow me to give you one more example that will help you understand practicing perfect love.

For years there has been one fear that I have not been able to deal with. This is the fear of elevators. When I began to see how powerful love was, I knew I needed to allow love to cast out this fear.

*Any potential
threat or cause
of pain comes
from someone
or something.*

No matter what anyone says or does to me I am a worthwhile person.

Any potential threat or cause of pain comes from someone or something. First, I determined what emotion I felt when I thought of elevators, the cause of my emotion. What did it make me feel? I felt fear. Did I want this feeling? No, I did not. Was it controlling me, and if so, in a positive way or negative way? Yes, it was controlling me in a negative way. Did I want to change this emotion so I would be in control? Yes, I did. Was this emotion limiting me? Yes, it was.

I made myself stand in front of an elevator. I stood there until I felt this fear. I began to see this fear as innocent, harmless, having no control over me. I thought: God loves me, I am free, I am not to be controlled by fear, I am love, love casts out fear. Peace is the ability to withstand anything that comes against me. I will direct the peace in me at this fear. When I felt this peace come back to me, I knew that it had touched this fear. Now I am at peace with this emotion. I am now free of this fear. I am able to forgive myself for being controlled for years by it. I am able to see it as harmless and innocent. As I love myself, I no longer allow fear to limit me. I am now able to get into an elevator. I am the one in control.

You love and forgive yourself when the cause is directed by something. You love and forgive the person when the emotion is caused by someone.

Because of a clear conscience, you are able to be at peace. This peace is directed at the threat until the threat is peaceful, harmless, or innocent. Now there is no reason not to love since there is innocence. This love forgives and frees from pain and bondage. The control is broken by our becoming in control when practicing perfect love.

Is there something or someone that causes you to feel threatened or painful? What emotion does it make you feel?

You love and
forgive yourself
when the cause
is directed by
something.
You love and
forgive the
person when
the emotion is
caused by
someone.

How does it control you? Do you want to change this control? If so, begin to feel this emotion. See the cause as innocent. Direct peace toward the cause. Feel the peace as it touches the cause. Now this cause of your emotion has no power over you. You see this someone or something as innocent. You can now love without any hesitation. You have forgiven because you have loved. You broke the control of this emotion. Now you are in control. You do not have this emotion or this pain. You are free. Love did cast out this fear.

All the negative emotions, such as guilt, resentment, bitterness, criticism, rejection and depression, are created by fear. Fear controls. Just as fear produces all negative emotions, love produces all positive emotions. We finally have two emotions that will control, love or fear. Each is very powerful and each will create a way of life for you. Love will create a positive life, and fear will create a negative life. It all comes down to your choice. Practicing perfect love is choosing a life that is full, rich and alive.

This perfect love helps us escape from pain, depression, sorrow and anxiety. When we are extending this love, we are making peace for ourselves and others. When we love, we do not abuse ourselves and others. This love is total acceptance and total giving without boundaries and exceptions. Love sees ourselves and others as blameless, absence of fear.

Practicing perfect love is the answer to the pain that is caused by the emotion fear and the effect of guilt and unforgiveness. You can love because you are love. Do not allow yourself to limit the power that has been given to you. You can love if you believe you can. Why experience a life of pain and sickness when you are being offered the answer to a life of peace? You must choose; no one can

*Fear controls.
Just as fear
produces all
negative
emotions, love
produces all
positive
emotions.*

Dr. Don Burchfield

I keep trying because there is hope.

choose for you. Please choose to discipline your mind to look at any area that would produce pain or hurt to you as an opportunity to practice perfect love. When you do this, you still find you are not getting upset or experiencing pain. The feeling you have is peace and a willingness to forgive and a desire to continue loving. Make the right choice and live an abundant life by <u>practicing perfect love</u>.

Once you truly understand how powerful love really is, your life can never be the same. When you actually begin making this concept part of your everyday life, you will be amazed at how you will feel. Being convinced that nothing that would provide a threat of producing pain can harm you, is life-changing.

When you can let go of the past and live now without the negative feelings from the past, you will become like a new person. This might sound too good to be true, but it is true.

Try each day to direct love at any situation that, if allowed, could bring pain to you. See how this love changes the effect. Become better acquainted with this concept as you practice each day. You will discover that practicing perfect love is the only way to live.

I remember when it seemed there could be no pain worse than what I was feeling. Life no longer had meaning. Everyone I loved was gone. I was all alone. The feeling inside left me so empty, so lost, seeking for someone to tell me that I would be alright.

Please, someone, hold me, tell me it will all be alright. Say words that will help stop these tears. No longer sobbing, just one tear at a time moving down each cheek. The aching in the middle of my stomach reminded me of my loneliness.

*Trusting the
power you have
found in love
and practicing
perfect love
will help bring
about your
healing and
allow you to
remain healed.*

Fear had driven me away from all that was part of my Life. Being convinced that I would never get well, I knew that it was a matter of time and I would cause my own death. Fear was in control and completely destroying my life.

If you are wondering if you will be able to experience the joy of life again, you will. I encourage you to apply what you have read. Trusting the power you have found in love and practicing perfect love will help bring about your healing and allow you to remain healed. This becomes a way of life. No longer do you just live life one day at a time, but you now live life at a level meant to be. Practice daily this concept and life will become more like what you have always thought life should be.

Knowing Truth

This message is a peaceful thought and feeling. It is the right thing to do. To experience this is a powerful message. When you experience something and it feels right even if it goes against the voices of people in your past, you should listen to the experience, which will not lead you wrong.

You cannot know truth until you have stopped telling yourself that you already know truth. You cannot understand until you stop thinking that you already know the truth.

The correct attitude is to be grateful, when becoming aware of a new and hopeful way to think.

When you're thankful in advance for that which you choose to experience in your reality, you, in effect, acknowledge that it is there. Thankfulness is the most powerful statement you can make.

*When you're
thankful in
advance for
that which you
choose to
experience in
your reality,
you, in effect,
acknowledge
that it is there.*

Self-care is not selfishness.
It is good for you.

It is not your function to create or uncreate the circumstances or conditions of your life. God created the process of life, and you create the rest. Your will for you is God's will for you.

You need not be concerned so much about the process as what the outcome will be. The ultimate outcome is assured. To doubt this causes fear and guilt.

All human actions are motivated at this deepest level, which are two emotions: fear and love. Humans will love, then fear, and destroy, then love again, motivated by fear. Listen to the fear. When you listen to fear and hear what it says, then you can prevent it. By preventing fear, you practice perfect love.

You might have been taught that when you are good, God is there, and when bad, He is distant. This cannot be true. Not even loving parents act like this. God's love is always there. You feel loved, then you worry, "I'll lose that love", and so you live in fear and guilt and not assured of unconditional love. There are no conditions set on this love, none at all. To practice perfect love is a its highest form when fear is gone and unconditional love is experienced for self and others.

God sees you as the most magnificent, most remarkable, most splendid of all creation. Why should He find fault in you, one who has an intent to please and love. This assurance rids one of fear, so perfect love can be experienced. When fear is gone, unlimited power is available.

There is no eternal banishment or damnation for anyone who considers God as the One to love. You cannot cause God to turn on you. There is just no way to run God off when you have a desire to love and be loved by God.

Listen to your feelings. Be true to what you are experiencing. Follow the thoughts and feelings that will bring the experience of love and not a fearful experience.

We have two choices: to love or to fear. We will do one or the other. That is our choice. We can fear or we can love, but we cannot do both. Question your thoughts Are they producing fear or love? Listen to your feelings. Be true to what you are experiencing. Follow the thoughts and feelings that will bring the experience of love and not a fearful experience.

Life is self-creative. You use life to create your self as who you are and who you want to be. To undo something, or change something, would be saying you no longer are "who you want to be". It does no longer reflect the new you. Change things in your life which do not fit into the picture that you wish to project into eternity.

To reduce pain is to change the way you behold the experience that you associate with what has caused pain. Nothing is painful in and of itself. Pain is a result of wrong thoughts. It is an error in thinking. Pain results from a judgement you have made about something. Remove the judgement and the pain disappears.

Judge not, and neither condemn, for you know not why a thing occurs, nor what the end result is to be. Remember that what you condemn will condemn you, and that what you judge, you will one day become.

When we are free from fear, we do as we please and experience the results of that. This gives us the chance to create the person we believe we are. Truth does this, so we can have the space to produce a higher self. We have free will. Free will to listen to the truth as we know it to be, or to continue to listen to what has been told from past teachers. To choose to stay in the past can produce a personal hell.

Hell is the pain you suffer from wrong thinking, the opposite of joy. It is knowing who and what you are and

*When we are
free from fear,
we do as we
please and
experience the
results of that.
This gives us
the chance to
create the
person we
believe we are.
Truth does this,
so we can have
the space to
produce a
higher self.*

Knowledge and understanding gives you back the power.

failing to experience that. It is being less. There is no need to fear revenge for failing.

Hell is when you separate yourself from your own highest thoughts about yourself. To deny who you are, to reject who and what you are. This is Hell. God does not ever deny us, ever!

We have no reason to fear. Fear is creation of self. We fear because of our fear, not of the fear of anyone else.

God has begun in us the process of life. We are to discover who and what we are by experiences. The process has begun to life will then have consequences, natural outcomes. What we think could be punishment is not evil, but nothing more than a natural law asserting itself.

The soul in you is complete, all sufficient, which is spirit. The soul knows the goal set for you at the beginning of life. The plan for you is in you, being realized from experience to experience. Each experience is to help fulfill the goal. Fear only prevents this. When you practice perfect love, you remove the fear that prevents you from allowing the experience to bring you one step closer to your goal being realized.

Direction is discovered from these experiences. The goal is set before you and the plan is to arrive. How you arrive is life revealed. There is no right way to get there. Each person will do different ways. The final plan is to get you to the goal, using whatever means needed to complete this goal, your journey called life. Fear, when allowed to, can prevent the goal from becoming complete. As you practice the steps of perfect love, fear cannot block your process of living your life as you desire it.

God has provided unconditional love and unlimited potential. This should help to reduce the fear tactics used by many to keep you under the control of certain beliefs.

*The goal is set
before you and
the plan is to
arrive. How
you arrive is
life revealed.
There is no
right way to get
there. Each
person will do
different ways.
The final plan
is to get you to
the goal, using
whatever
means needed
to complete
this goal, your
journey called
life.*

What would God need to punish if he provides no conditions to His love? Why would God need to punish when the natural outcome of wrong thoughts and wrong choices provide punishment in themselves?

Nothing happens by accident. There is no such thing as a coincidence, even though we may call it that. Things all happen for a reason. Things happen because of our thoughts or choices. When we think we had nothing to do with what happened, we are very much involved. The goal and plan set up at the beginning is being revealed. Thoughts or actions for the plan and goal to become reality. Remember, all has been provided at the beginning to make sure the goal established will become a reality at the end. Your part is to be open to love's power and be willing to resist what fear would like you to believe.

You have come here to work out your individual plan for your own salvation. Not salvation from punishment, but the saving of yourself from not believing and continual processes of life. Save yourself from the many temptations to quit moving ahead. You will not fail or lose this battle called life, if you do not stop trying. Make sure you keep listening and following the direction you find from the many sources available to you each day. Your salvation is in the belief that life is yours to create and to live out in true fulfillment, knowing you are living as you have hoped.

Remember there is no coincidence and nothing happens by accident. Each event and adventure is called to yourself, by yourself in order that you might create and experience who you really are.

When you begin to fear that you are not following truth, listen to the fear. There are no conditions on acceptance of love. You are pleasing when you simply are wanting to. To

*Remember, all
has been
provided at the
beginning to
make sure the
goal established
will become a
reality at the end.
Your part is to be
open to love's power
and be willing to
resist what fear
would like you
to believe.*

be waiting for yourself to fail so you can be punished is guilt and fear attempting to rob you of love.

Good Happens

Here is a daily task, take inventory of where you are and where you want to be. Then begin to change. Consciously change your thoughts, words and actions to match the vision or goal. You will want to monitor yourself. You will want to take inventory as you travel on your journey. This is a conscious choice that produces change.

For some to believe something good should happen is difficult. When good happens, people begin to prepare themselves for the bad to come to wipe out the good, because, well, they just do not feel they deserve the good or feel it is too good to be true.

For some, it could be hard to believe; but the truth is, you are goodness, mercy, compassion and understanding. You are peace, joy and light. You are forgiveness, patience, strength, courage and a helper. You are wisdom, truth, peace and love. You are all of these and more.

Before you arrived on the scene, the universe had principles it developed from the beginning. These principles do work. They are part of the universe in which you live. People will not be aware that they are causing these principles to work, because they might not be aware of them. To be aware or not is not necessary, because these principles are still active. The wonderful truth of these principles is that, when you know how they work, they become exciting to the ones who are aware.

*For some to
believe
something
good should
happen is
difficult. When
good happens,
people begin to
prepare
themselves for
the bad to
come to wipe
out the good,
because, well,
they just do not
feel they
deserve the
good or feel it
is too good to
be true.*

Creating Your Reality

You are part of creation. You create as you were created. Creation begins with a thought. Creation then moves to a word. You have heard, "Ask and you will receive", "Speak and it will be done". Creation will then move to deed, which is the result of your thought and the speaking of the word. The created deed is manifested in your reality. This deed does manifest itself as you believe it can. This is, again, another way for you to understand how practicing perfect love can be achieved.

When you have this gut-level clarity that this is the truth, begin then to be thankful for this that you have created with your positive energy. This positive energy you sent out does, and will, come back to you as positive. To know this as true, is the key. To know you are sure is the confirmation of your creating powers that you have tapped into.

You do create your reality. When you are clear about what you are thinking about, creation begins. Think about what you want to be, to do, or to have. Think on this often, only do not doubt or wonder or fear. The "I am" is creating the strong emotion swelling up inside as you believe. The "I am" is the center of your being, which is a summation of all you believe yourself to be.

This operating process is not anything to fear. There is an excitement to know all has been provided when you were created. Now you are to create just as you were created. You are not an accident, and your thoughts are not for you to waste. They are there to create as you were created.

*You do create
your reality.
When you are
clear about
what you are
thinking about,
creation
begins. Think
about what you
want to be, to
do, or to have.
Think on this
often, only do
not doubt or
wonder or fear.*

We reduce the power of the past when we talk about it.

Continue along your journey from stop to stop to monitor your thoughts. To monitor is to take inventory of your actions. Do you act as one who is a creator of his own reality? Do you act as a servant to life or are you the creator of the life you live? Take inventory of your actions which only are a mirror to your attitudes and beliefs.

Life is a process. When life brings you to a stop in the journey, it is then you are to create. You will know why the stop was planned. Remember, the plan and goal was established from the beginning. You have been stopped so you can create, and then you can move on. Think about it!! As you practice this plan of perfect love, you create all that is good and destroy the bad that could block your goal. Keep in mind the goal and continue to create.

Creation with a purpose. The saying "What goes around, comes around". This is more than a saying. You can stake your life on this. This will become a reality. This is creation. What goes around is the thoughts and actions, spoken into reality, which will come back as reality. When one sends out negative, evil, self-motivation, egotistical, ugly and rude thoughts, you can be assured these same thoughts will return as reality to the one who created them. You do not need to ever think negative thoughts of others so they will receive negative results. These will only come back to you. The one who sends thoughts out will reap the reality of these thoughts in time. Trust this, rest in this, and do not create your own form of revenge through thoughts. For you alone will suffer the results, not the one who you thought about.

You will always get what you create. Others will always get what they create. Life proceeds out of your intentions for it. When something happens, ask yourself, "Did I, at anytime, think or hope what is now happening?"

*As you practice
this plan of
perfect love,
you create all
that is good
and destroy the
bad that could
block your
goal. Keep in
mind the goal
and continue to
create.*

You will find, at sometime, that which is happening is what you hoped for.

Creative Thoughts

Anyone who reads these words will feel a sense of freedom and excitement. However, one of the first thoughts that will come to you is "How do I escape the thoughts I have now learned to think?" The key here is 'learned'. Just as you learned thoughts that drain, you can re-learn and un-learn. Keep reading these truths that give you a sense of hope. As you repeat these thoughts, they will remain and the other thoughts will not surface. The thoughts you feed are the thoughts that become stronger. The same goes for those you do not feed. They become weaker until they die out. Feed the thoughts you choose to have and they will create in you even more positive healing thoughts that will lead you to the person you were created to be. Believe this, because it is the truth.

God is love. God is all that is love. To accept that God loves you is not being weak. All of us want to be loved. We all want to be needed. To accept that God loves you can only be a good thing. This same God is responsible for creation. Creation has begun with you and your life. Accept that you are the one given the responsibility to create as you were created. God is your partner, not your reminder of how imperfect you are. God works with you to create. Step out in this life and create without fear of not being good enough or that you will be punished.

The thoughts, attitudes, beliefs, and ideas you have at this time may not be consistent with what you have just read. Not to worry, these are supposed to be a part of you.

*As you practice
this plan of
perfect love,
you create all
that is good
and destroy the
bad that could
block your
goal. Keep in
mind the goal
and continue to
create.*

These have been the results of years of experiences and a lifetime of encounters. They are not what you want to continue to carry with you. New thoughts can be re-learned and un-learned as mentioned before.

Here is a reminder of three steps, which are thoughts, words, and actions. You think the thought you want to become part of reality. Now that you have the thought, speak it into words. Begin to do or act on these words as often as you can. This new thought and action now becomes part of you as it is repeated. This will drown out the old thoughts. Fear is now something you can overcome. Yes, as you practice perfect love, fear is cast out.

You can create new thoughts that produce life that reflects the person you want to be or you can continue allowing old thoughts to keep you from evolving.

If allowed, thoughts will repeat themselves without any control. They will just run in a vicious circle. Thoughts lead to experiences, which lead to thoughts, which leads to experiences. You are what you think you are. Break in that circle and stop the thoughts that you do not want. If you do not act and allow thoughts to go off on their own, you will remain defeated. <u>Act</u> now before you <u>think</u>. Act quickly and follow with your new thoughts and new actions. Act before the mind tells you this is wrong, because it will. The mind is used to one way and to change it takes determination. <u>Change your mind</u> about what your mind tells you to do. Determine now, right now, to <u>change your mind.</u>

I am changing my mind. That is the first step. Decide now that you will change your mind. No one does anything he does not want to do.

Now what? First, do not get frustrated and think you will never be able to believe what you have been reading.

*You can create
new thoughts
that produce
life that reflects
the person you
want to be or
you can
continue
allowing old
thoughts to
keep you from
evolving.*

This would be a natural response. Take this booklet and read it over again and again. I have found that, the more I read these words, the easier it becomes to believe I can follow these steps of Practicing Perfect Love. Please give it time, and please do not give up.

When we keep trying, we are making changes, even if we are not aware at the time. Little changes, one at a time, become big changes when they are all added up at the end. You can do it, just take time and create a new way of thinking that will make life the enjoyable adventure it was first created to be.

The first paragraph stated that you can be free from the control of your past experiences and thoughts, and live in peace and joy today. This has been given to you in a step-by-step plan. The hope is that you now know this life is for you, and you will now live a life of "perfect love".

APPENDIX

- Being afraid of being afraid = anxiety.

- Control the uncontrollable = worry.

- Worry thinks 'if only', 'what if'.

- Worry is a problem when it interferes with the life we live.

- Where you put your mind is where you put your time.

- Reward for patience is patience, the body responds in a non-anxious way when patient.

- Pain = I see what I want, I think I can't, I get angry, I push it down, I get anxious, I get depressed.

- Wrong thoughts create wrong actions.

- On-going dealing with forgiveness/anger.

- Anger is resentment, bitterness = anxious.

- Life is a great adventure or nothing at all. What we think is what we get.

- Change your mind, change your life.

- Disease-fighting cells are affected by emotion.

- Life a process, dealing daily, becomes a lifestyle, not crisis management but crisis prevention.

- Be where you are at when you are there.

- To value control can be anxious-producing.

- Choose to react and respond to what is happening around you, in a negative or positive way = anxiety.

- Fear-anxiety-fear-anxiety, etc.

- Choosing to do nothing causes anxiety.

SYMPTOMS OF DEPRESSION

Have you had:

1. Sad mood longer than a week?
2. Sleep disturbances, unable to go to sleep, wake up a lot?
3. Change in school performance or work performance?
4. Somatic complaints (stomach, head, back)?
5. Loss of usual energy, fatigue, tired most of the time?
6. Fear of failure, not wanting to try, making excuses?
7. Feelings of inadequacy, saying "I can't do it, so why try?"
8. Look to be sad or unhappy, mentioned by others?
9. Self-deceptive thoughts, negative self-image, hated self?
10. Aggressive behavior, acting out, not cooperating?
11. Reduced socialization, withdrawal, feeling comfortable alone?
12. Change in attitude toward school or work, bored?
13. Unusual changes in appetite or weight (gain or lose)?
14. Feelings of being unloved and not likeable, feeling that no one cares?
15. Low frustration tolerance, easily irritated?
16. Self critical, saying, "I am no good. You would be better off without me?"
17. Rebellious, arguing back, resenting advice?

18. Disobedient, irresponsible, ceasing to do regular chores?
19. Substance abuse (drugs or alcohol use increased)
20. Over-emotional, cries easily.

IF YOU ANSWERED YES TO FIVE (5) OR MORE, COUNSELING IS RECOMMENDED.

WHAT DO YOU FEEL?

- Do you feel you need to be punished?
- Do you feel you will never get another chance?
- Do you have one conflict after another?
- Do you feel you are not worth being loved?
- Do you feel that you push away people you love?
- Do you feel that others would rather be with someone else than with you?
- Do you find yourself putting up a wall so no one can get through to you?
- Do you feel that you cannot trust love?
- Do you sometimes fear going to sleep because, when you wake, you just hurt even more?
- Do you feel isolated from family, parents?
- Do you react to change?
- Do you feel you are bad?
- Do you feel that others are unhappy when they are with you?
- Do you feel that there is no hope?
- Do you feel that you are being controlled by something other than yourself?
- Do you find that you feel guilty, but don't know why?
- Do you have physical and emotional problems?
- Do you think of different ways to die?
- Do you feel that your life doesn't matter?
- Do you stop trying because you might fail?
- Do you expect a lot from yourself?
- Do you feel that you don't belong?
- Do you feel that you don't know who you are?

- Do you feel that, if you get close to someone, something bad will happen to him or her?
- Do you feel that there is hate within you?
- Do you want to punish yourself?
- Do you feel that, since you hurt, others should too?

If you answered 'Yes' to 7 or more of these questions, counseling is recommended.

IRRATIONAL BELIEFS

1. If I fail on this task, I am a total failure.
2. People will laugh at me and despise me forever.
3. I will never succeed (after this failure).
4. How can I ever be happy after this defeat?
5. I must not make a mistake if I want to succeed.
6. I can only accept a perfect performance.
7. If people give me compliments, they don't mean it.
8. My good shots were luck.
9. I should have never made this stupid decision.
10. I must not fail.
11. I should always feel satisfied.
12. It is mean that they are laughing at me.
13. Life is rotten.
14. I must excel.
15. I am worthless if I appear stupid or weak.
16. I must be approved by my friends.
17. I have to be popular.
18. I should always feel loved.
19. I got rejected, so I must be unlikable.
20. I must not feel lonely.
21. People must treat me fairly and give me what I need.
22. It is terrible if people don't live up to my expectations.
23. People who act immorally are rotten.
24. I can't stand bad things and difficult people.
25. I can't stand it when things don't go my way.
26. Life is not fair to me.

INFORMATION PACKETS

<u>Order No</u>. <u>Name of Packet</u>

1. Youth Suicide Information
2. Depression Among Adolescents
3. Thinking Adolescent, Drugs, Sex and Violence
4. Children Who Can't Pay Attention (A.D.H.D.)
5. Anger Packet (Children and Violence)
6. Anxiety Info & Techniques to Treat, including Childhood Anxiety
7. Posttraumatic Stress Disorder
8. The Adolescent, How he Thinks, Summary of Adolescence
9. Self-Esteem Communication Skills
10. The Age of Stress, The Impact of Divorce
11. Parenting Packet
12. Early Childhood Development, Power of the Brain
13. Information on Schizophrenia/Serious Mental Illness
14. Information on Borderline Personality

Dr. Burchfield has compiled information packets on the above subjects. Order by the order number and how many of each packet. Send $5 for each packet to: C. A. M., 4547 North 17th Avenue, Phoenix, Arizona 85015. PLEASE SEND MONEY ORDERS ONLY.

Dr. Don Burchfield

<u>YOU CAN</u>

If you think you are beaten, you are;
If you think you dare not, you don't;
If you'd like to win, but you think you can't;
It's almost a cinch you won't.
If you think you'll lose, you've lost
For in this world you find
Success begins with person's will—
It's all in the state of mind.

If you think you're out-classed-you are;
You've got to think high, to rise;
You've got to be sure of yourself before
You can ever win the prize.
Full many a race is lost
Ere ever a step is run;
And many a coward fails
Ere ever his work's begun..
Think big and your deeds will grow;
Think small and you'll fall behind;
Think you can and you will—
It's all in the state of mind.

Life's battles don't always go
To the stronger or faster man;
But sooner or later the man who wins
Is the fellow who thinks he can!

Affirmations for Self-Esteem

What I Am

I am lovable and capable.

I fully accept and believe in myself just the way I am.

I am a unique and special person. There is no one else quite like me in the entire world.

I accept all the different parts of myself.

I'm already worthy as a person. I don't have to prove myself.

My feelings and needs are important.

It's O.K. to think about what I need.

It's good for me to take time for myself.

I have many good qualities.

I believe in my capabilities and value the unique talents I can offer the world.

I am a person of high integrity and sincere purpose.

I trust in my ability to succeed at my goals.

I am a valuable and important person, worthy of the respect of others.

Others perceive me as a good and likable person.

When other people really get to know me; they like me.

Other people like to be around me. They like to hear what I have to say and know what I think.

Others recognize that I have a lot to offer.

I deserve to be supported by those people who care for me.

I deserve the respect of others.

I trust and respect myself and am worthy of the respect of others.

I now receive assistance and cooperation from others.

I'm optimistic about life. I look forward to and enjoy new challenges.

I know what my values are and am confident of the decisions I make.

I easily accept compliments and praise from others.

I take pride in what I've accomplished and look forward to what I intend to achieve.

I believe in my ability to succeed.

I love myself just the way I am.

ANXIETY

When anxiety is kept within tolerable limits, it can be an effective stimulant to action. It is a normal response to an unknown danger, experienced as discomfort, and helps the individual mobilize his resources in meeting the problem. As anxiety increases, however, perceptual awareness narrows and all perceptions are focused on the difficulty.

If a solution is not found, anxiety may become more severe. Feelings of discomfort intensify, and perceptions are narowed to a crippling degree. The ability to understand what is happening makes one unable to recognize one's own feelings, the problem, the facts, the evidence, and the situation in which he finds himself.

The goal would be to reduce the anxiety enough to enable one to belting solving the problem.

Reduce the discomfort by learning how to cope, reduce stressors, return to a balance, and the anxiety and tension will be at a level that is tolerable.

Golden Rules for Coping With Panic

1. Remember that although your feelings and symptoms are very frightening, they are not dangerous or harmful.

2. Understand that what you are experiencing is just an exaggeration of your normal bodily reactions to stress.

3. Do not fight your feelings or try to wish them away. The more you are willing to face them, the less intense they will become.

4. Do not add to your panic by thinking about what "might" happen. If you find yourself asking, "What if?" tell yourself "So what!"

5. STAY IN THE PRESENT. Notice what is really happening to you as opposed to what you think "might" happen.

6. Label your fear level from zero to ten and watch it go up and down. Notice that it does not stay at a very high 'level for more than a few seconds.

7. When. you find yourself thinking about the fear, CHANGE YOUR "WHAT IF" THINKING. Focus on and carry out a simple and manageable task.

8. Notice that when you stop adding frightening thoughts to your fear, it begins to fade.

9.   When the fear comes, expect and accept it. Wait and give it time to pass without running away from it.

10. Be proud of yourself for your progress thus far, and think about how good you will feel when you succeed this time.

Seven Steps To Building
High Self-Esteem

Help people to:

1. Recognize they are beautiful and unique just the way they are.

2. Get away from believing they have to stack up with others.

3. Recognize that self-worth is innate; it's not determined by actions and decisions.

4. Become more responsible for their choices and decisions.

5. Recognize mistakes are stepping stones to achievement.

6. Recognize that life is a journey to be embraced one day at a time.

7. Recognize that praise pays-even when things aren't going well.

DEPRESSION

- Persistent sad or "empty" feelings

- Loss of interest or pleasure in ordinary activities,

- Chronic fatigue

- Continuing sleep disturbances (insomnia, early-morning waking, or oversleeping)

- Change in appetite causing weight gain or loss

- Difficulty concentrating, remembering, making decisions

- Uncontrollable feelings of hopelessness or guilt

- Irritability

- Thoughts of death or suicide

- Chronic aches or pains that have no physical basis

- Persistent comments from family and friends that you are not acting like yourself.

ATTITUDE

By Charles Swindoll

"The longer I live, the more I realize the impact of attitude on life.

"Attitude, to me, is more important than facts. It is more important than the past, than education, than money, than circumstances, than failures, than successes, than what other people think or say or do.

"It is more important than appearance, giftedness or skill. It will make or break a company...a church...a home. The remarkable thing is we have a choice every day regarding the attitude we will embrace for that day.

"We cannot change our past...we cannot change the fact that people will act in a certain way. We cannot change the inevitable. The only thing we can do is play on the one string we have, and that is our attitude.

"I am convinced that life is 10% what happens to me and 90% how I react to it. As so it is with you...we are in charge of our ATTITUDES."

ABOUT THE AUTHOR

Don Burchfield has his Doctorate in Psychology. Don has been an Adolescent and Family Counselor since 1974. Don started a non-profit organization called *Advocates Against Adolescent Suicide*. The organization provides free training and seminars to help reduce the depression among the youth. Don has presented the material in this booklet at the *Solutions for Families Conferences* since 1995. Don has written other programs called "Give It a Day" which helps young people think before they act.

For more information, call 1-602-861-1121